RUNNING A WEB DESIGN BUSINESS FROM HOME

~

How To Find and Keep Good Clients and
Make Money with Your Home Business

ROB CUBBON LTD
LONDON SW1

Running A Web Design Business From Home
Rob Cubbon
Published by Rob Cubbon Ltd., London. *http://robcubbon.com*
© 2014 Rob Cubbon
ISBN-10 1494366282
ISBN-13 978-1494366285

Contents

Introduction

Summer 2005 was particularly hot here in England. The London underground trains during the evening rush hour could reach temperatures of 40ºC (104ºF). The air was thin. The commuters were tired. Even worse, on July 7th terrorist bombs had killed scores of people on those tube trains. The atmosphere was hot, tense and angry. I used to take those trains.

I used to try to read a book rather than infect my mind with the evening paper. But it was hard concentrating. Every so often the carriage would lurch, it was noisy, there wasn't much time between stations. I used breathing techniques, affirmations, guided meditations to try to relax. But it's hard to achieve the serenity of a Zen master in Finsbury Park.

In Finsbury Park I would leave the train tunnels to journey further through endless pedestrian tunnels before I finally reached daylight in order to take a bus to my flat. It's not that life was hard; life was *meaningless*.

If commuting was meaningless, my work wasn't any better. I was working at design studios and marketing companies in central London. I was supposedly in a creative industry but creativity seemed stifled by the corporate structure and office politics. Too many designers would spoil the client and I didn't have the patience.

When I look back to those times it's hard to think of myself as the same person. It's not as though the memories are painful. I was truly bored, directionless and, yes, unhappy. It's so hard to see how, in such a short amount of time, I made a massive difference to my life. But I'm going to explain this. And I'm going to explain how you can affect this change on your life too.

If you're working for a company or boss you don't really care for. Or if you do care but think your efforts would be better directed towards your own company then read on.

If you've made steps towards running your own business but need help in pushing it up to the next level, then this book's for you as well.

The most important thing I did was to start a blog. Check it out: *http://robcubbon.com.*

All I did was write honestly about what I was doing and this has opened up a wealth of opportunities.

I continue to blog to this day and I would like to invite you to follow me on my journey by signing up to my newsletter at *http://robcubbon.com/free.* You'll only get a few emails and you can unsubscribe at any time. You'll also receive two free e-books, *How to Market Yourself Online* and *Starting An Online Business.*

There is actually very little difference between freelancer and CEO; between Mac monkey and entrepreneur; between employee and employer. It's just a few switches in your brain. It's subtle but it's profound.

Let's get going!

What's in this book?

This book will explain the basics behind setting up and running a web design business from home.

Just because we're at home, doesn't mean we're going to get comfortable, watch daytime TV and play around with our pets all day. I'm going to explain how to think of yourself as a business and that's going to involve some work.

I'm not going to teach you how to design – *one of the secrets of running a design business is that you'll spend less than half your time designing!* – but I will explain all the necessarily starting steps, processes, software, hardware and systems you'll need as well as explaining how to avoid some of the pitfalls.

And, we'll have fun too! It's not all about hard work.

ME

My name's Rob Cubbon. I've been running a successful web design business for over six years. I'm not the greatest designer in the world. The success of my company in these uncertain times is probably more down to good business sense than anything else and that's what I'll attempt to impart to you.

During all this time, as I say, I've been keeping a blog and I'll recommend that you do the same. Starting a blog was the best business decision of my life and it's the reason why I'm able to write about this subject. If you want to run any sort of business from home you should start a blog. I'll explain about this later.

BUSINESS MODEL

Please be aware this book is about how to run a business that makes money. Making money is what businesses should do. You won't be satisfied with your business if it's not making money so that is the starting point. Next, you should enjoy your business – when you wake up in the morning, you'll want to start working your business. And, finally, you should be focussed on providing the best possible service for your clients.

We are now, hopefully, coming out of the worse period of recession since the 1930s. But, I didn't feel it. People that own their own businesses typically have been lean and nimble enough to avoid the worst of the bad times. This trend will continue. Jobs for life in large organisations are harder to get.

Working from home on your own business is not only more satisfying, it is also a safer option long-term. It will provide you with a useful skillset that you will keep adding to as the years go by. You will also learn to adapt quickly to the changing environment into order to capitalise on new opportunities as they emerge. Larger companies will not be able to compete with you.

My design company, Rob Cubbon Ltd., prides itself on providing high quality design and marketing solutions for its clients. It's very different from being a "freelance web designer" who swaps hours for money. I think of myself as a business not as a guy who gets paid for making websites and you should do the same.

I also pride myself on forging mutually beneficial long-term business relationships. This is also very important. Almost every second of the day I'm forming new relationships, through my blog, through my email list, my social media, the meet ups I go to, etc., even now, I'm forging a new business relationship – with you!

Business is all about relationships and I love meeting people online and off. So, you know where to find me, drop me a line and hook up if you're in town!

THE WEB DESIGN BUSINESS

The web design business worldwide is huge. Everybody needs a website. And everybody needs online marketing

I have contacted many other independent web designers. And, by canvasing a range of opinions along with my own experience, I can give you the great advice about how to embark and prosper in this exciting industry.

Would you like to run your own? Do you want to know how to get started or how to improve your business? I hope so because one thing's for sure: **you can do it.**

Will you have to work hard? Yes, but think about the millions of people who work in factories, shops, call centres, etc., they work pretty hard and get little satisfaction from their jobs. However, someone who runs their own business is *always* satisfied with their work.

We've all heard the statistic that 50% of all new businesses fail within their first year – don't let this bother you. You can start running a web design business with zero risk. I was freelancing in London, working through agencies and going to offices and studios. I was getting paid by the hour to do repetitive print design tasks.

I found it easy to work on my web design business in the evenings and weekends. As the business grew I took less and less freelancing work on. Until, two years later, I was ready to work on the business at home full time. If the business failed I could have easily gone back to freelancing. I still could. Zero risk, you see!

What you need is a solid plan so that you *don't* see yourself as a freelancer – swapping hours for dollars – but so that you see yourself as a business.

I want to take you on a journey so you can see how to run a business without working all the hours God sends and gaining the financial freedom you deserve. I wish you much happiness and success with your own web design business.

RUNNING A WEB DESIGN BUSINESS

Setting up my own web design business from home was the best thing that ever happened to me.

I got home from work one day and told myself that no short-haired, yellow-bellied son of Tricky-Dicky is going to mother-hubbard soft-soap me with just a pocket full of hope. Thanks to John Lennon for that wonderful turn of phrase. I actually think I might have put it stronger than that!

Running a business

Here is my business model based on my years of experience running a design business. Remember, there are three things I've tried to do with the business over the years: have fun, provide a great service for my clients and make money.

The objective of every business is to make money and this should always be at the back of your mind. It's incredibly easy to get caught up in the details and not to see the bigger picture. So the first thing you should do when you are starting a business is to make sure you're not wasting time or money.

HOW TO SAVE MONEY WHILE RUNNING A BUSINESS

Of course, you will have to spend money on software and hardware. But you should be strict with yourself about expenditure. Here's what I mean:

- Don't use your mobile for calls, use free apps
- Buy second-hand or refurbished equipment when you can
- Don't spend money on professionally printed headed note paper, etc., send invoices out electronically as PDFs and let the client print them out if they wish (however, I will let you purchase professionally printed business cards!)

- Be wary of potential clients who ask you to meet them before they've given you any work, and certainly never work for free (unless you're starting out and it's a great client).
- Ask yourself "do I really need this" before making an investment in the business. If you believe it will improve your business then make the purchase, otherwise not.

This is especially true with marketing and advertising where it's easy to waste time and money. I would advocate you market yourself by putting all your energies into your website and blog rather than doing anything else.

I have found that all necessary promotion can be done using a blog, basic SEO practices, social media and by developing on- and offline business relationships. All this costs no money at all and I'll explain this later.

However, you can skimp and save too much. If you do have the money then always invest it to grow your business. So, if you have a slow computer, you should definitely buy a better one. This is a business investment and the money will be well spent if you are getting clients and getting paid. And the expense can be deducted from your revenue that you pay tax on – so it means you pay less tax.

Another example: don't struggle with boring repetitive tasks if you have enough money to outsource them using services like Elance and oDesk. There's a time to save money and a time to spend money. Obviously, spend it once it's coming in to facilitate making more of it; don't spend it when you're starting out and haven't got it. Everything in moderation, even moderation.

HOW TO SAVE TIME WHILE RUNNING A DESIGN BUSINESS

Saving time is just as important as saving money. There are a hundred and one little jobs to do when running a web design business so it's really important you're strict with yourself as far as productivity is concerned:

- **Always use email rather than phone.** Even if you are slow at typing, emailing is usually a time saver. An email creates certainty. Clients can see what you're saying in "black and white" plus there's a record of what's been said. Phone conversations are two-way and therefore so much more likely to create confusion. Sometimes the phone or Skype is necessary but most of the time it's not.

- **Create distinct time blocks for certain tasks.** Get rid of distractions in the work environment: noise, the dog, phone, etc., shut down Twitter, Facebook and email and resolve to complete tasks in time. You may like to block of 25 minute or 45 minute periods for work before taking 5 minute breaks, but then get back to work.

- **Always ask yourself this question:** "Is what I'm doing right now getting me where I want to go?"

HOW TO DELIVER QUALITY WHILE RUNNING A WEB DESIGN BUSINESS

So once you have the saving money and saving time mindset firmly in place, you now need to concentrate on how to deliver quality to your clients.

Your business must be a premium service. There are plenty of design businesses out there. You need to compete on the basis of quality and NOT on the basis of price. There will always be companies out there that will beat you on price and if you fall into that trap there's very little hope of getting out of it.

So how do you offer quality? Is it just a case of having a beautiful portfolio and telling the client "I offer quality"? No. It's all about communication.

COMMUNICATION. COMMUNICATION. COMMUNICATION.

Further on in this book I will explain how to sell to a client websites, logos or other design by offering pre-made packages. If a potential client contacts you wanting a website, for example, you can take one of your pre-made packages "off the hook" and present it.

The beauty of this system is that you can show the client that you're more than just a freelance web designer to hire but you run a successful digital solutions company that covers all areas of the online space.

Creating systems will also increase productivity as you'll have the processes written down and be able to perform it off pat. You'll also be able to outsource the tasks to others easily. I'll show you later how systems are the secret to a smoothly running successful business.

People will contact you wanting a website but 9 times out of 10 they won't have thought about SEO, social media, a blog and sometimes even content. You need to offer as many of these services as possible.

People are lazy. Time and again, I have set up blogs, social media accounts and email marketing for clients and they've never got round to using them. They purchase fantastic methods of getting their message out there and then do nothing with them.

Incredible, but true. And, this is why you have to create and offer as many of these services as you can. Most clients want someone to take away the confusion, hard work and effort away from them. And, if they get quality with it, they will pay a premium.

So, remember communication between you and the client is key. If you can sell systems to your clients rather than just services you will be more successful. And it requires communication to sell systems. We'll find out how to do that later on.

Starting a web design business

All you really need is a computer and an internet connection and you can start a web design business. But, of course, it's not as simple as that.

Try, wherever possible, to utilize the equipment and communication infrastructure you already have rather than rushing out to the stores. Remember, we're trying to get the money coming in here, not the other way round! And as I've already said, struggling along with a slow computer is a false economy.

COMPUTER

Whether you are a Mac or PC person, you will need a fairly decent computer with large disc space, fast processor and bags of RAM.

At the moment, I'm sitting behind a 27 inch iMac with 3.2 GHz processor, maxed out 16 GB of RAM and a 1TB hard drive. Yes, it's a beast. It's actually already two years old and the chances are you could be reading this in a year's time thinking, *who does this guy think he is, asking us to run a web design business with such out-dated tech!*

It's frightening how quickly computers increase in power and become more affordable. Suffice to say, you'll be buying new equipment every other year, if not most years.

However, with something like this iMac, you'll have all the computing power and speed needed to get you going and the hard drive will be more than enough to store your work at first. Laptops, tablets and smartphones are pretty essential for today's web designer but, again, don't go crazy. Don't buy every device out there for testing purposes.

SOFTWARE

In order to do design work, you're going to have to get some software. There's a lot of great free and open source tools out there that, in some cases, do the job as well as the expensive stuff. But, for graphics, unfortunately, you pretty much have to get the Adobe Creative Suite, or Creative Cloud, as it's now called.

To get the Creative Cloud you have to pay a monthly subscription which for an individual will be somewhere in the region of $50 a month (in the UK much more, about £47/month).

If the above subscription is too much for you, you can look on Ebay for a computer with a version of Creative Suite already installed. Or get reductions on Creative Cloud if you qualify as a student or a teacher.

The 3 applications I use the most are Photoshop, Illustrator and InDesign. I also like to use Acrobat Professional and Premier Pro. I also like Dreamweaver, but it's not essential for creating websites there are free text editors and an FTP clients you can use.

If print designers have too many fonts open it can cause decreased performance in their machine. You could open and close fonts manually or you may like to purchase a font management program that will open and close fonts for you optimizing your computer's speed. I use Suitcase Fusion 3 or you could use Linotype FontExplorer. For websites however, you'll mostly be using Google's free webfonts service.

Don't purchase loads of fonts. Wait until the work comes in first, and then, if you can't find any good free fonts, purchase a few of your tried and tested favourites and charge the expense to the client. And, have a look, there are loads of great free fonts out there.

ON-SITE BACK-UP

Further down the line, you'll have your hard drive stuffed with client work, software and not to mention your photos and movies. What happens if something should go wrong with your computer? You need back up and a portable alternative.

The cost of external discs keeps going down and down. You can get a decent 1 or 2 TB external hard drive for $60 or $90 or so.

If you run a Mac, all you have to do is to set up Time Machine and all your work will be backed up so that if you deleted something a few days ago you go back in cyber time to retrieve it.

You should also consider a cloud-based back-up system like Dropbox or Google Drive.

OTHER FREE TOOLS YOU CAN USE

Open source alternatives to Creative Suite. Free open source versions of Creative Suite applications exist but they are no real substitute. GIMP – the open source equivalent of Photoshop – has been around for a long time and is definitely the best alternative but, frustratingly, not as good as the real thing.

File Sharing. If you want to deliver large files to a client there are a host of free services, I use Dropbox and Google Drive. All these cloud services have paid options for more space.

Images. There are lots of places to get great free stock photography: stock.xchage *http://www.sxc.hu/*, RGBstock *http://www.rgbstock.com/* and Flickr Creative Comms search are amongst my favourites.

There are loads of free vector resources but, instead of searching through these resources, I find a Google image search for "free vector" usually does the trick. Likewise, it's not always necessary to get a free vector logo from Brands of the World but just google the brand you want with "vector" in the search query.

Fonts. You can pick up free fonts at DaFont and a host of other places. WhatTheFont can identify a font from an image. As already mentioned, as far as web fonts are concerned, Google Fonts now has a catalogue of over 600 excellent fonts that will work across most browsers with just a line of code in the head and a CSS declaration. Compare and contrast the fonts with TypeTester.

Grids. If you like to use grids in your web design (or even if you don't) then check out 960 Grid System *http://960.gs/* where you can download grid templates in HTML & CSS, Photoshop, Illustrator, GIMP, etc. All these grids are for websites that are 960 pixels wide.

Web developer tools. These are a standard fare for most web designers you'll find yourself using these tools many times a day. You can access Developer Tools for Chrome, Safari, Firefox and Internet Explorer by Control-Shift-I (Command-Option-I on the Mac) to inspect and change HTML and CSS and help you de-bug JavaScript. Developer Tools on IE is great for working out IE hacks. Developer Tools on Safari helps you with designing sites for the iPad and iPhone. I used to use Firebug – an awesome Firefox add-on that does much the same thing as these Developer Tools.

Also there are web developer add-ons for Firefox and Chrome which can disable styles, disable browser default styles (handy for cross-browser compatibility), show alt text for images, resize window, etc. The HTML Validator and the CSS Validator can be reached with one click using these add-on services or you can access them via the browser.

Other online services of importance to the web designer are **Google Analytics** and **Google Webmaster Tools**. These are fairly essential to any website owner.

Cross browser checks. I'm pleased to say that I don't check sites across different browsers and devices nearly as much as I used to since I started developing with the Genesis Theme Framework on WordPress. But you can check websites across different browsers at BrowserShots. ViewLikeUs checks a website in the most popular resolution formats.

Speed. In order to analyse your page speed, use Google's PageSpeed (try to get your score as near to 100 as possible) and Yahoo!'s Y!slow.

Downtime. Use Pingdom's free service to be instantly informed of downtime so you can sort it out as soon as possible.

Color. Color Scheme Designer can help you choose complimentary colors for your website designs. And Adobe's excellent Kuler lets you browse, search, and modify color themes directly in your browser.

The best things in life are free, as they say. It's very difficult to know where to start and where to stop in compiling a list like the one above. Some online free services are so ubiquitous you forget to add them to a list like this – for example, WordPress and YouTube.

KNOWLEDGE AND ABILITY

You won't find out how to design websites by reading this book, I'm afraid. However, I've recently surveyed a lot of web designers and asked them how they learned. There were three main ways of learning web design, and one of them is quite surprising – by reading books!

The first and main way to learn web design is, surprise, surprise, by designing websites. It's frustrating, but the best way is to start by creating the HTML and CSS yourself. You may like to develop static HTML sites at first. Although they may have little commercial benefit, static sites will teach you some best practices.

You should try to learn as much about WordPress as you can – especially theme development. In my opinion, WordPress is the best CMS for creating websites for small and medium sized companies. Later you can explore plugin development, PHP and JS. There's a lot to learn and you'll have your own interests and specialties.

During this initial learning phase you'll be profiting from the second way to learn web development – from the internet. Whenever you find yourself up against a website brick wall, and you will frequently, you can search for the answer online amongst the plethora of tutorial sites, documentation and forums. I've lost count the amount of times I've been helped by one of the many nameless, faceless souls there are that help people out with web design issues. I try to give back online as much as I can because of the amazing help that I've received on web design forums.

In addition to practical experience and online research you can learn web design and development by reading books on it and taking courses.

But, don't give up! Web design is fantastically frustrating at first but quickly rewards hard work. Pretty soon you'll be answering those questions on forums and wowing people with your geekiness.

You will need a certain amount of technical knowledge. You will know how you can help people. However, there will always be a limit to your know-how. And, while you'll want to do as much as you can yourself at first, you'll also need to develop a network of trusted freelancers and friends you can outsource to as well.

This doesn't mean contracting freelancers from oDesk or Elance to work while you take all the credit. But, remember running a web design business is not the same as being a web designer. You have to be the CEO, COO, the marketing manager, the financial expert and ship's captain so, if you see any sort of success, you'll need to off-load some work to others.

HAVE A PLAN

All businesses have to have a business plan. In fact, on a personal level, creating goals is a great practice for us all.

You should be thinking about the direction and the ultimate destination of your company. Think of the clients you'd like, the projects you'd want to be involved with and the sort of work you'd like to be doing day-by-day. Business goals aren't just for the initial stages of a company. It's important to have long-term and short-term goals.

The goals can cover the quality of work you are doing, the amount of new business you are getting, traffic to your site, the amount of profit you are making and, most importantly, how you're going to *enjoy* yourself.

Make sure the ends justify the means. If your goal is making money, make sure you enjoy the process by which you believe you'll make money. Otherwise, you'll spend your time doing something you don't want to do in order to make money. This is stupid.

Make your plans as SMART as possible – that is specific, measureable, achievable, realistic and timely.

It doesn't even matter whether you achieve these goals or not. Thinking about them, writing them down and trying to actualise these goals has tremendous benefits.

Goals give us focus and something to aim for – otherwise you can easily get swamped in the day-to-day running of the business. But there's much more besides. I believe the practice of writing down a specific goal actually makes it more likely to be realised!

You should also a "mission statement" or simple philosophy that sums up your business.

OK, I'm going to beg now (I ain't too proud). Please don't ignore this part of starting and developing a web design business. Constantly writing down your goals is something you have to do if you are going to be a success.

STARTING OUT

Do I sound pretentious by saying "the best way to start is to start"? Yes, I thought so.

Sometimes people can fall victim of analysis paralysis. We'll all suffered from that particular condition at some stage. But, web designing for clients is something that can be done at home by anyone with a computer and an internet connection. Accountants can be sorted out later; the company name can be sorted out later; even the business plan can be thought about and sorted out later (but not much later!).

If you've got a full time job you can start in your spare time and leave setting up the company until later. Or if you do have time on your hands – now is the best time to start an online business. And designing from home is a fantastic way to make money.

At some stage, you will have to have a proper company set up with it's own bank account, accounting, (and, not to mention, logo, website and email address). You should do all this sooner rather than later.

But the most important thing to start with is with your own website. And we'll get onto that in the next chapter.

Getting work

Probably the question I get asked most often is how do I get clients? Many people often ask me about freelance sites such as Behance, oDesk and Elance. Is this the way to make money as a web designer? The answer is no. Sites like these will always benefit the consumer (the clients) rather than the producer (you). You will make less money.

Clients will be the lifeblood of your business and the best way to get them is through your site.

BLOGGING

The best way to get clients to your site is by blogging. You could advertise and hire SEO agencies if you wanted to but you'd be chucking money down the drain.

I'll be coming on to this later in the chapter but I am an unapologetic proponent of blogging. If the one thing you do as a result of reading this booklet is to start a blog or to re-double your blogging efforts, then I have helped you more than any of the other advice you'll receive for the next year.

It is that important. Blogging improves your brand recognition, teaches you marketing, teaches you about your business, helps you meet people and gets you traffic. And, that's not the half of it.

Your own blog with good on-site SEO and incoming links will get you better clients than any freelance site ever will. This will take a bit of time but it's better to get clients coming to you rather than the other way round.

Everything starts and finishes with your website. You should be working on it and looking to improve it almost every day. You can engage with social media and forums, etc., but use them for driving interest to your own site. Your site should be the hub of your online world.

Why would potential clients contact you from your website? Because you create quality content about what you do. You should write about everything you can possibly think of in your particular area of expertise. Drill down into your specific talents and write about them in minute detail.

So, don't just write about web design. Write about, for example, multi-lingual e-commerce sites, android apps with geo-tagging, case studies of companies you've helped in a particular area. More specific titles attract more specific readers. Pretty soon, you'll get clients looking for specific skills through the search engines.

And, don't stop there. Take the time to research into related areas you don't know much about. Writing a tutorial is incredibly educational. People will start to arrive at your site from search engines, see you know what you're talking about and hire you. But, remember, make sure your content is as good as it can be. This is your online reputation and your business depends on it long term.

What software should you use to create your website? I can hear you laughing because there's only one answer: WordPress.

Although WordPress comes with pretty good SEO straight out of the box, there are some essential SEO actions you need to perform. These are basic things like putting your keywords in your site title, headings, subheadings and URLs, creating a sitemap and registering it with Google Webmaster Tools, writing meta descriptions for pages and alt tags for images. There is plenty of information out there about on-site SEO and you could probably fill a few Kindle books talking about it. However, it's pretty straightforward and if you're stuck you could ask on forums or ask me at *http://robcubbon.com/contact* or *rob@robcubbon.com*.

You should also optimize certain pages for keywords. You can write certain blog articles according to your specialisations. So, for example, a blog post entitled "How To Create A Multi-lingual E-commerce Site" is targeting people who are using the keywords "multi-lingual e-commerce" in searches. The most important on-page ranking factor is the title, so put the keywords in there, in the subheadings, in the text – but only where it's natural. With SEO, never do anything unnaturally. So don't stuff keywords in to titles or anywhere else. If it reads funny, it looks funny to Google and that's bad.

The keyword to target for your home page maybe "web designer *blank*" where "*blank*" is the city or area you live in. You can tailor this to your own requirements, maybe "web app designer *blank*" or "graphic designer *blank*" or even "freelance web designer *blank*" would be a better keyword for you. Whatever you decide on, you should put those keywords in the title of your home page and occasionally variations of them in the titles of your blog posts.

Another factor of huge importance to search engine ranking and SEO is inbound linking. As I'm sure you know, the more links you have pointing to you from relevant, high authority web pages, the better. How do you obtain these links? Well, creating content that people are going to want to link to is a start.

After that you will have to promote your content using social media and your circle of friends on the internet. We'll get on to relationships later but maintaining a close-knit group of friends that are designers and professionals in related fields is essential to any web design business owner.

So, if your blog's constantly updated with relevant content and has relevant social signals and relevant links pointing to it, you will get targeted traffic.

Back to the keywords again, further oomph to your pages can be gathered by the anchor text of the links pointing to them. The anchor text is the actual words that comprise the hyperlink. So, if you have a link to your home page with the anchor text "web designer *blank*" then that will increase your ranking for that keyword by a greater or lesser extent, depending on the authority and relevance of the page with the link.

But, **be careful: do not mess around with anchor text!** Do not have more than 20% of links pointing to any page with the same anchor text – if the anchor text is something other than the title or URL of the page. A couple of years ago, people found that they could rank quite easily if they engineered multiple links back to their home pages with the same anchor text. Google got wise to this in 2012 and the infamous Penguin update wiped out many internet marketers' income overnight.

You may wonder how this concerns you as the links pointing to your site are on other sites and therefore not under your control. However, when setting up profiles and writing guest posts you can determine anchor text so it's important to be careful. When in doubt, use your site's domain name as an anchor text as you can't go wrong with that.

It's also good practice to have links pointing towards your internal pages as well – portfolio pages as well as blog posts.

I can not overstate the importance of blogging. Blog as much as you can, write relevant quality articles of at least 700 words as often as possible. Get yourself into a rhythm. Publish once a week, twice a week, everyday. Any interval is OK but keep it regular. And don't forget to put the keywords in the titles of the posts.

You can monitor your success with online tools such as Google Analytics and Firefox addons such as Rank Checker.

It can actually become quite addictive. You can monitor where your visitors are coming from, what they do on your site and how you're ranking for certain keywords on Google. After a while you'll develop a sixth sense for what works and what doesn't and you can tailor your articles to attract the sort of visitors you want.

So that was a very quick introduction to blogging.

YOUR PORTFOLIO – LESS IS MORE

Just like your blog, your portfolio will require constant attention. Although, I spend more time on my blog than on my portfolio.

It's important to remember that prospects will spend very little time on your portfolio. They want to see examples of your work –

and they want to see them quickly. You should present your work samples in the best and fastest way possible.

It's up to you how you do this. I like to show screenshots of websites which link to the functioning site as well as thumbnail images of other work that present a larger version in a JavaScript "lightbox" when clicked.

Always try to narrow down the number of samples of your work that you show. It's better to see only 5 fantastic websites rather than 55 ordinary ones.

STAND OUT FROM THE CROWD

Above all, be creative and break the mould. Always try to offer something different from everybody else.

One of my favourite web designers, Paul Jarvis, never reads web design blogs or follows the work of other web designers and, as a result, creates very original websites and is in constant demand.

Try to take on work that you love doing – follow your bliss – and be constantly asking yourself "is this good enough to put in my portfolio?"

Don't be afraid to put "made up" work in your portfolio. It is perfectly acceptable to create a website for a fictitious company in order to showcase your very best design skills.

PUT YOUR USPS, SKILLS AND SERVICES ON YOUR BUSINESS STATIONERY AND EMAILS

Your clients and prospects may not always be aware of the services you offer. I have "Marketing materials, Print, Branding, HTML

Email, Website design & development, hosting & maintenance" in my email signature. So that anyone receiving mail from me will know that I don't just do web design.

Write down a list of services you offer. Think of all the places where potential and current clients could see this list. I put a list of services on my email signature, invoices and letters.

NEVER TURN DOWN A GOOD JOB

If someone asks for a job you can not do – think about it. Don't just say "no". If it's a job that you would be completely at sea with then, of course, you'll have to turn it down. But if, for example, the job is a WordPress site – but with a membership, multilingual or e-commerce element – and you are confident designing and developing in WordPress, then I would advise you to take it.

You have to be very careful with this – only accept the jobs that you know you can complete satisfactorily. Elance and oDesk are good for finding contractors to help you with tricky areas of the job, if you don't know of anyone personally.

This is a win-win-win. You increase your expertise, develop a relationship with a new contractor, get a new client and get paid. (And don't forget to write a blog post about what you've learned.)

NEVER TURN DOWN A GOOD CLIENT

Great clients may start off with tiny jobs. Don't do all manner of jobs for rock bottom prices.

However, if it's a good client, you should take the job no matter what – even if it's very small. I wouldn't bother doing small jobs (less than 100$) for some clients. But if it's a good client then the job is worth doing.

THE BEST CLIENTS ARE YOUR CURRENT CLIENTS

I surveyed over 40 independent graphic designers, and most of their work comes from existing clients or recommendations from existing clients.

This is why it is difficult or almost impossible to start a full time web design business from home straight away. You have to start part-time, in the evenings and weekends, and build up this all-important client base. Once you start to get good clients you'll realise the importance of maintaining great relationships with them.

FORM PARTNERSHIPS AND ALLIANCES WITH OTHER WEB DESIGNERS

Today business is all about connections – online and offline. Continually nurture professional relationships with other designers, illustrators, developers, etc. You can meet people and forge relationships through social media, your website or through meet-ups in your local area.

Whenever you can, upload your designs and ask for comments and advice via social media. This can be scary, but by showing a little bit of vulnerability you can create some excellent connections. Try to help people who ask for advice whether on social media, through forums or directly through your inbox. How do you find these connections online? Twitter is very popular with designers and there are some excellent LinkedIn, Facebook and Google Plus groups. And there are forums: for example Estetica Design Forum, Graphic Design Forum, Designer's Talk, there's Digital Point and Sitepoint for more code/technical queries and the WordPress forum is excellent.

Some designers see success from searching Twitter, Facebook and looking on these forums for web design jobs in their area. I personally haven't done this but I can see how it could be fruitful – and it is certainly better than getting work from bidding sites.

Getting meaningful connections with other web designers and professionals will teach you about the industry and benefit you in numerous other ways. However you should try to limit your time on these social networks as they can be distracting.

My second favourite way to find clients is from face-to-face meet-ups. Every major town or city has regular meet-ups of business people. Web designers are lucky – we don't have to find specific industry meet-ups. We can meet potential clients at any business group.

These business and networking meetings are not only for finding clients. They are a great way of getting away from your computer and talking to other professionals. You can discover partnerships and joint ventures opportunities that you weren't even looking for. Try MeetUp.com *http://www.meetup.com* or BNI to find them.

IF YOU'RE JUST STARTING OUT

Don't worry about picking the "right day" to start your own business. You can start today! Of course, I'm not suggesting that you leave a steady job when you don't have any clients. But you can take the first steps whilst still in employment. Anyone can start up their own business, you just need a business bank account, an address and a couple of hundred dollars.

Creating a business and a website can be your first steps. You can do this whether you are employed, semi-employed, unemployed or retired. You can work for your very first clients in your spare time. You can carry on building up your client base for years before running your own business from home full time.

So the best time is now – there has never been a better time to start your own design business.

Clients

At first, the success of your business will depend on your ability to attract good clients.

Remember, not all clients are created equal. Good clients are long-term business partners that will provide you with regular income and recommend you to other good clients. Bad clients will actually cost you money.

CHOOSE YOUR CLIENTS

When you are starting out, you will be tempted to work for any client whatsoever. However, you will quickly learn that some clients are better off left alone.

You will want clients that are honest, straightforward and, better still, part of a large company or organisation. You won't want to work for clients who are lazy and dishonest.

There are a number of "red flags" that I listen out for in order to identify bad clients. For example, I would tend to avoid clients who say things like, "this won't take you long", "if you do this for free there's a guarantee of future work" or "can you write a proposal on how to improve these 4 websites".

The relationship with the client is based on mutual respect. If a client doesn't value your time at the start, don't expect them to in the future.

Don't take any sort of client. Don't look desperate. To a certain extent it pays to "play hard to get". Good clients are a win-win. They pay more and treat you better. A bad client knows you will do anything for a little money, so they will treat you badly and pay less – if at all.

CHOOSING THE RIGHT COMPANIES

You don't always have the ability to choose, but if I could choose a company to work with it would be a large organisation. As a web designer working for a lone entrepreneur is great, but you'll have to find a lot of them to make a reasonable amount of money.

However large organisations are more likely to provide recurring income.

One of the companies I work with is Accenture, a Fortune 100 company with over 225,000 employees. I did a job for one person there in 2006 for £500. Fortunately he was happy with the job I did and recommended me to a colleague. Now, I probably know 20 to 25 people in that organisation and do several jobs for them every year.

So, if a large company like Accenture contacts you, don't be picky! Move heaven and earth to do the best job you possibly can for them.

Larger organisations may be more bureaucratic and smaller companies may be more creative. But, for me, an on-going relationship with a large company provides a solid foundation for your web design business.

TREAT EVERYONE IN THE SAME WAY

Even though, as I say, not all clients are created equally, I always treat everyone with the same respect and politeness. This is because, I believe, I am a brand. Everything I do reflects on my reputation and my business. So whether I'm talking to a CEO or and intern, or emailing or on Skype, I will always try to be true to my core values.

ALWAYS BE POSITIVE

Conversations with clients can be frustrating. They don't always ask you to do what you want to do for them. However if the client suggests a course of action that you don't believe to be the right one, always meet the suggestion with positivity.

Start by pointing out the advantages before explaining the drawbacks. Never use words like "difficult", "delay", "complicated". Always be positive and, as long as you are sure you can help the client, do everything with a smile on your face.

If you haven't read The Seven Habits of Highly Effective People by Stephen Covey, you should. Here is something the late, great Stephen Covey wrote in his blog:

> "The key to being proactive is remembering that between stimulus and response there is a space. That space represents our choice – how we will choose to respond to any given situation, person, thought or event. Imagine a pause button between stimulus and response – a button you can engage to pause and think."

Your first reaction to what the client says may not be the best.

LISTEN, LISTEN, LISTEN

In the end interaction with a client comes down to one thing – listening. You can be the greatest web designer in the world but, if you can't listen to clients, your company will amount to nothing. Ask questions and listen to the answers. Many people can be very good at talking about their website idea but not very good at explaining the actual purpose behind it. It is the job of a web designer to turn a dream into reality. You need to ask the right questions in order to find out exactly what the client requires.

The website can be the most integral part of somebody's business. So communication about the site should be purposeful, exhaustive and then written down. Both parties should agree on what needs to be done and this should be set out in black and white.

GET THE LANGUAGE RIGHT

It is not safe to assume that all clients have prior technical knowledge. To some people, web designers speak a foreign language so it is essential to understand the client's technical know-how.

BALANCE

Overall it's necessary to strike a certain equilibrium between being flexible on one hand and not too easy on the other; between working with good clients on one hand and not turning down too many on the other; between being positive on the one hand and realistic on the other.

If you love solving problems and love the clients, you will go a long way.

Handling projects

Being asked to do a great project for a fantastic client – there is nothing quite like it! I remember the buzz the first time I got the call. And I still get the same buzz today.

However, that's the only similarity. Otherwise, there are no two website jobs that are exactly the same. Some of them aren't even websites – I get asked to do presentations, apps, email, print design, you name it – but I'll talk about diversification later.

As I've already said, communication is key. Understanding what the client requires is almost half the battle.

Sometimes you have to distinguish between what the client asks for and what they actually need. Often clients get so excited about the look or functionality of the website that they forget about attracting visitors.

You need to discover the purpose of the website – does the client want to sell products, obtain email addresses or market their brand. You may have to delve deep into your client's core values to find this out.

AUTOMATE THE PROCESS

A secret to running a successful business is to set up systems and automate the process.

It's easier to explain this with an example: If a client wants a website, you will have a document prepared listing exactly what you can do. You can copy and paste elements from this document and send it to the client with the price as a proposal.

Having tasks and procedures written down makes projects easier to complete and, ultimately, is easier to automate and outsource.

The sooner you start to do this the better. Next time you have a job open up a text file and list the various tasks performed in order to undertake it. This'll make it easier the next time you perform this task.

Furthermore, you can expand these task lists into blog posts and YouTube videos. Publishing your processes like this will help you in various ways.

Quality blog posts will attract visitors to your website. Quality blog posts that helpfully explain a process will increase your authority – both with the search engines and with your visitors/ prospects. You can also use these YouTube videos and processes to help with your outsourcing.

EDUCATION

Often you will be explaining to the client what works online. There are extreme examples of this: a client can ask for a 5 page website and expect traffic to come automatically. That maybe rare nowadays, but some clients do need to be educated about the best ways to achieve their aims.

Some clients may not know about WordPress. You will have to educate them to use WordPress. Again, create YouTube videos to tutor your clients to do certain things. (Mac users, buy Screen-Flow to create these videos, PC users can use both ScreenFlow and Camtasia.)

An email subscription list is one of the best ways to create interest in you brand and build a following, but many people don't realise this. As web designers we are in a unique position to suggest tools and actions that clients would take years to discover. However the trick is to persuade the clients to make these steps.

LEAVE NO STONE UNTURNED

Once you understand your client's core values and what they want to achieve with the website, now proceed with baby steps. By this I mean show the client your progress every step of the way.

First show the client a visual that you have mocked-up in an image editing application (Photoshop). Get the client to agree to a visual of the homepage or one other important page of their new website. This will ensure a more seamless development process.

GET THE CLIENT INVOLVED

Unfortunately some people think websites can be left alone – I call this the "set it and forget it" mentality. You need to explain to clients that a website is a living and breathing thing – it needs to be constantly updated. The work on a website never stops.

The best way to engender a hands-on approach from the client is to get the client to enter as much content as you can. Engage the client during the development process by asking them to create or edit certain pages in WordPress. This ensures that the client learns the necessary skills in the right way. Sometimes the client will enjoy this process and it will mean less work for you!

Don't just be a web designer!

Even if you charge $2000 per website, you'll have to find a lot of clients in order to make enough money.

That's why we spoke earlier about getting large corporate clients who provide regular work. But there are many other opportunities to augment your income both actively and passively.

Another reason why you are incredibly lucky to be a web designer is that there are so many related skills branching out from the core discipline. For example, people who want websites I'll also likely to be interested in online promotion.

There are a host of other services you can offer your clients:

HOSTING AND MAINTENANCE

I've started with the most common form of recurring income a web designer can earn. However it is also potentially the most fraught. We haven't the time and space to talk about this completely, but here are a few pointers.

If you want to host your clients' websites, only do so on a web server you really trust. Try not to get involved with email but, if you do, root the email through Google Apps for Business.

As always, be completely clear with the client what you will be providing and what you won't be providing. And, finally, always charge top dollar for this service – make sure it's two or three times more than the client would be paying if they did it themselves. If something goes wrong, hosting issues can take time to sort out.

TEXT EDITING AND COPY CHECKING

Some clients may appreciate help with text. If you see text that you believe needs editing, and you are comfortable doing this, you can offer this as a service.

Very often all it needs is the next pair of eyes checking the spelling and punctuation.

WRITING

Another benefit of blogging is that it improves your writing abilities. Having to write a blog post every week makes you a better writer. Some clients will be happy to pay extra to have their text improved.

SOCIAL MEDIA

It's quite likely that somebody requiring a new website will also require social media profiles set up. Many of these profile pages (Twitter, Facebook, Google Plus, etc.) require header images, background images and profile images.

A web designer can easily offer to create these images or set up the social profiles for the client.

PRINT DESIGN AND OTHER DESIGN SERVICES

I am actually a print designer turned web designer. So I am happy to provide other services such as business cards, flyers, brochures and on-screen presentations.

This provides a significant part of my annual income. So I would advise web designers to diversify the services they offer as much as possible.

WEB DESIGN AND PASSIVE INCOME

As a business owner you should always be looking to increase your streams of income. Many of these extra income streams will be passive income. Active income is when you do a web design for a client – the income depends on your hourly labour. Passive income, on the other hand, is income you can earn in your sleep. Here are just a few ways a web designer can earn passive income:

- **Advertising**. Don't get carried away with this one. Even if you have a successful blog you won't make much more than $50 a month with advertising. And I would caution against putting ads prominently all over your website.
- **Selling WordPress themes**. Once you can bend Word-Press to your will, you can make a lot of money by selling your own themes. You can do this either through your own site or throughput third party sites like Themeforest.
- **Selling icons and vectors.** We slave away for hours and hours on Illustrator creating icons or illustrations for our clients. But some of us never consider that we can be paid more than once for the same job. The quality needs to be high when submitting to sites like Shutterstock and GraphicRiver.
- **Selling info-products**. There is potential to great money with e-books and video courses. Once you have found a great niche and audience through your blog you can begin to make money with these sorts of products. I have

been particularly successful selling video courses through online learning platforms like Udemy.

- **Software as a service**. This requires technical know-how which you'll probably have to outsource. However, if you find a problem within an industry, software as a service can be sold on monthly prescription.

SPECIALISATION

On the one hand you have to diversify on the other you need to specialise. Make sure you enjoy what you do. Being naturally drawn towards jobs that inspire you.

Follow your bliss!

Be happy!

What could be better than doing something you love every day? I enjoy designing and I enjoy providing a good service to my clients. I also love blogging and helping people market their businesses.

Nothing would make me happier than if this booklet could help you in some way. Maybe it could help someone leave a job they hate and start their own web design business.

Honestly, if it helps only one person, it would be worthwhile. Working on your own business is 10 times better than working on somebody else's.

So, this is the end of my booklet. I really enjoyed writing it and I hope you enjoyed reading it as well!

Maybe you felt inspired to start your own web design business. Maybe you already have a web design business and this booklet has helped you in some way. If so, I would really appreciate a review on Amazon, or anywhere else for that matter. The more stars and more positive reviews I get, the more we will be able to help others experience the liberation of working for themselves.

If you have any questions please pop along to my website and leave a comment on one of the articles or drop me a line at *http:// robcubbon.com/contact*.

All the best to you, your family and your business!

Further reading

If you enjoyed this book there are a few others I can recommend for you:

- *Get Graphic Design Clients: Pro-tips for Landing, Impressing & Keeping the Good Ones* by Wes McDowall
- *Work for Money, Design for Love: Answers to the Most Frequently Asked Questions About Starting and Running a Successful Design Business* by David Airey
- *Manage Your Day-to-Day: Build Your Routine, Find Your Focus, and Sharpen Your Creative Mind* by Jocelyn K Glei
- *Creative Workshop: 80 Challenges to Sharpen Your Design Skills* by David Sherwin

The above books can be found on Amazon.

Special offers just for you!

As a token of my appreciation to you for reading my booklet, I would like to offer you the following online video courses at half price or less!

If you're interested in setting up and running a web design business from home then each of these three courses will help you in a different way. The links goes straight through where you can purchase the course at a discount or there are discount codes which you can enter at the checkouts on Udemy.com.

Running a Web Design Business. Access this course through the special link *http://robcubbon.com/offer29* to get the course at a 57% discount. The course explains how to make money from home designing and developing websites for clients. About how to get clients, how to handle clients, how to organise projects, contracts, specialisation, etc. It goes into much more detail than this book does. There are also sample invoices, contracts and proposals to download.

Creating a Business Website with a Responsive Design. Access this course through the special link h*ttp://robcubbon.com/ offer34* to get the course at a 56% discount. This course contains 4.5 hours of tutorials showing the building a web design company website with WordPress and Genesis (you have to get the Genesis framework ($60) for this). This shows you everything from the beginning to the end: from design in Photoshop, transferring the PSD to WordPress as well as local and remote development.

Build Your Brand: Blogging, SEO, Social & Relationships. Access this course through the special link *http://robcubbon.com/ offer24* to get the course at a 59% discount. This is probably the most useful course I've created. It explains everything I've done to get over 1000 visitors a day to my site. It explains blogging, social media, on-site SEO and how to build those all-important business relationships to make sure you get noticed as an expert in your field.

Please let me know if you have any questions about any of the courses.

http://robcubbon.com/contact

Legal Disclaimer:

This report is not intended to be a source of legal, business, accounting, or financial advice. It is based on the personal experiences and observations of the author. Readers are encouraged to seek out the services of competent professionals for such advice.

The author and publisher have made every effort to supply accurate and thorough information in the creation of this report. But, they offer no warranty and accept no responsibility for any loss or damages of any kind that may be incurred by the reader as a result of actions arising from the use of information found in this report.

The author and publisher reserve the right to make any changes they deem necessary to future versions of the publication to ensure its accuracy.

The reader assumes all responsibility for the use of the information within this report.

If you do not accept the terms of this agreement, please return the product immediately for a full refund, at which point you must destroy any copies of the publication in your possession.

Peace!

Made in the USA
Lexington, KY
15 January 2015